PRESCHOOL

101 Things to Know About MATH

quack

Written by Marilee Robin Burton

active minds®

Marilee Robin Burton is a freelance educational writer, consultant, and language-arts specialist who holds an M.A. in early-childhood education and human development. She has more than ten years of experience as a teacher and is a contributing author of *365 Ways to a Smarter Preschooler*, *365 After School Activities*, *365 Reading Activities*, and *Circle Time Activities*. Her work has also appeared in *Parenting*, *Creative Classroom*, *Early Childhood Today*, and a number of other publications.

Illustrations by George Ulrich, Patrick Snan, and Ted Williams
Cover photography by Siede Preis Photography and Brian Warling Photography
Additional images by Adobe Systems, Inc., and PhotoDisc, Inc. Copyright 1999.

Louis Weber, C.E.O.
Publications International, Ltd.

7373 North Cicero Avenue
Lincolnwood, Illinois 60712

Ground Floor, 59 Gloucester Place
London W1U 8JJ

Permission is never granted for commercial purposes.

Customer Service: 1-800-595-8484 or customer_service@pilbooks.com

www.myactiveminds.com

ActiveMinds® is a trademark of Publications International, Ltd., and is registered in the United States.

8 7 6 5 4 3 2 1

Manufactured in China.

ISBN-13: 978-1-4127-9959-1
ISBN-10: 1-4127-9959-7

Contents

Add Some Fun to Math

Dear Parents:

Preschool is an exciting time for children. They are ready for new challenges, such as learning to read and write letters and numbers, recognizing shapes, and learning to count. They seem to want to know more about everything! Of course you want to give your child that special head start that is so important.

This workbook will help your preschooler learn the basic skills of a vast array of math concepts and processes—skills your child will build on in the future.

Inside this workbook children will find fun-filled math activities right at their fingertips. Each activity focuses on a different skill and provides your child with plenty of opportunity to practice that skill. The activities are arranged in order of difficulty, beginning with the most basic skills in order to build your child's confidence as he or she goes along. Children will feel a real sense of accomplishment as they complete each page.

Every activity is clearly labeled with the skill it teaches. You will find skill keys written especially for you, the parent, at the bottom of the page. These skill keys give you information about what your child is learning.

Children learn in a variety of ways. They are sure to appreciate the bright, colorful illustrations in this workbook. The pictures are not just fun—they also help visual learners develop 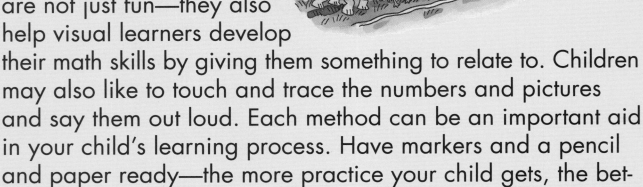 their math skills by giving them something to relate to. Children may also like to touch and trace the numbers and pictures and say them out loud. Each method can be an important aid in your child's learning process. Have markers and a pencil and paper ready—the more practice your child gets, the better. He or she will enjoy putting these new skills to work.

You can help your child by reading the directions for each exercise aloud before he or she completes it and by reviewing your child's work afterward. Each activity will be fun and enough of a challenge that it will be engaging for your child. Be patient and support your child in positive ways. Let your young learner know it's all right to take a guess or pull back if unsure. And, of course, celebrate the successes. Learning should be an exciting and positive experience for everyone. Enjoy your time together as your child enhances his or her preschool math skills.

Pick a Pair!

Draw lines to connect each pair of objects that are the same.

Skill: Matching like pairs

7

Making Tracks!

Whose print is whose? Draw a line to connect each animal's hoof, foot, or paw to its print.

Skill: Matching like items

Look-Alikes!

These twins like to dress alike.

Color their outfits so they are the same.

Skill: Coloring to match

Funny Faces

Draw lines or dots to make each pair of faces the same.

Skill: Drawing to match

Where's My Mom?

Help the baby animals find their moms.
Draw a line from each baby to its mother.

Balloons for All!

Give each child a balloon.

Draw a string from each balloon to a child.

Draw 1 more balloon for the last child.

Skill: 1-to-1 correspondence

Ready for Rain

Who's missing what?

Draw a line from each child to the rain gear they are missing.

Pizza Party

Is there enough for everyone?

To find out, draw a line from each child to a piece of pizza!

Was there enough? Check 1 box.   Yes   No

Parents: Children can build 1-to-1 correspondence by touching objects as they count them. Ask your child to double-check the answer by counting the children and the pieces of pizza.

Skill: Using 1-to-1 correspondence to determine quantity

Fruit Count

Are you hungry? There is a lot of fruit here.

How many apples? Circle the correct answer.

1   2   ③

How many oranges? Circle the correct answer.

1   2   ③

How many bananas? Circle the correct answer.

1   2   ③

Skill: Counting to 3

15

Jumping Through Hoops

Dixie jumps through a hoop when Dave counts to 5.

Help Dave count from 1 to 5. Trace the numbers as you count.

Ready, Set, Go!

Help start the race.

Count backward from 5 to 1.
Then, say, "Go!"

5   5
4   4
3   3
2   2
1   1

Skill: Counting backward from 5 to 1

Hide and Seek

Help Sam count to 10 so the other children can hide.

1   2   3   4   5   6   7   8   9   10

Then, count the 10 hidden children as you help him find them! Once you have found them, mark an X through them.

Skill: Counting to 10

Something's Fishy!

Color the picture using the color key.

Color the shapes labeled #1 blue.

Color the shapes labeled #2 green.

Color the shapes labeled #3 orange.

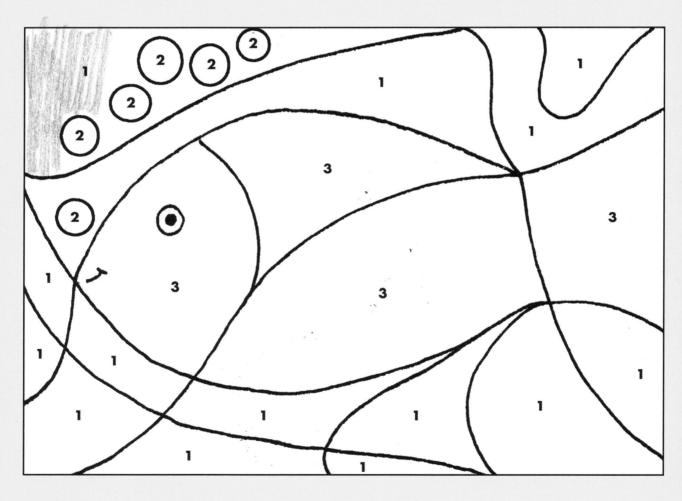

Skill: Recognizing numerals 1–3

20

Building Castles

Circle 1 crab.    Circle 2 shovels.

Circle 3 seashells.

Skill: Connecting numerals 1–3 with quantity

Finding 4s and 5s

Circle each 4 you see.

Draw a square around each 5 you see.

Skill: Recognizing numerals 4 and 5

Play Ball!

Color the players on team 6 red.

Color the players on team 7 yellow.

Skill: Recognizing numerals 6 and 7

Backyard Bugs

Circle 4 butterflies.

Circle 5 snails.

Circle 6 worms.

24

Skill: Connecting numerals 4–6 with quantity

7 Silly Stars

Color the number 7.

Color 7 silly stars.

Skill: Connecting the numeral 7 with quantity

What's Hiding?

What is hiding in the picture? Color the picture using the color key to find out.

Color the shapes labeled #8 blue.

Color the shapes labeled #9 green.

Color the shapes labeled #10 orange.

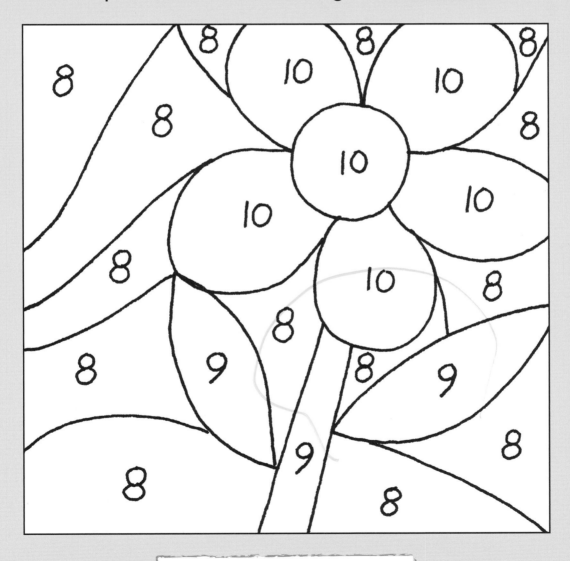

Skill: Recognizing numerals 8–10

Fabulous Fruit

Color the 8 apples red.

Color the 9 bananas yellow.

Color the 10 oranges orange.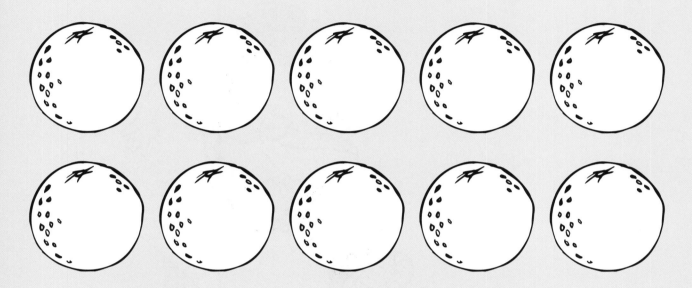

Draw and color 1 picture of your favorite fruit!

Skill: Connecting the numerals 8–10 with quantity

Park Play

Connect the dots from 1 to 5 to complete the picture.

Skill: Sequencing numbers 1–5

30

What Comes Next?

What number should go in the box? Draw a line to show.

1 2 3 ☐

4 5 6 ☐

3 4 5 ☐

6 7 8 ☐

9

4

7

6

Parents: Children may also want to write the missing numbers in the boxes.

Skill: Completing patterns to sequence numbers

31

What Comes Before?

What number comes before the 3 numbers in the fish? Color the bubble to show.

Big or Little?

Is this zoo animal big or little?

Connect the dots from 1 to 10 to find out.

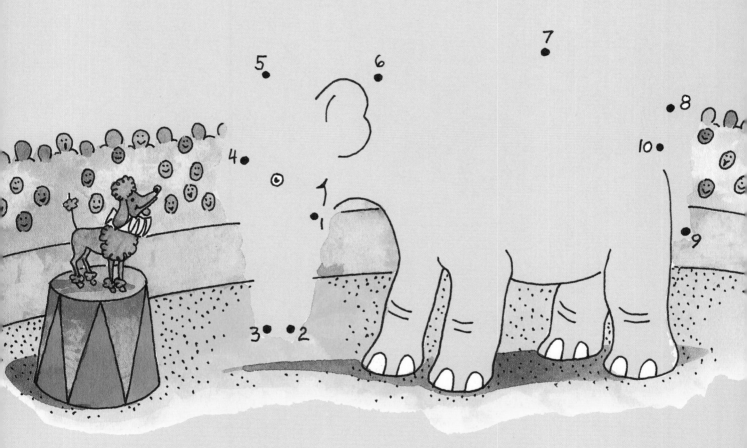

Carriage Ride

Draw a line along the number road to lead the carriage to the house.

Parents: Ask your child to name the numbers as the drawn line passes them.

Skill: Recognizing and sequencing numbers 1–15

Tasty Treats!

Count the treats in each picture.

Circle the number that tells how many.

2   4   3

2   1   3

3   2   1

4   3   5

Button Up!

Look at the number under each jacket.

Draw that same number of buttons on the jacket.

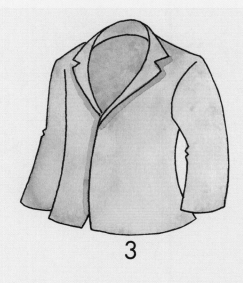

3

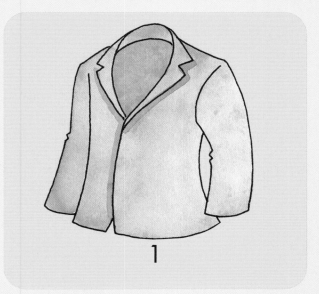

1

2

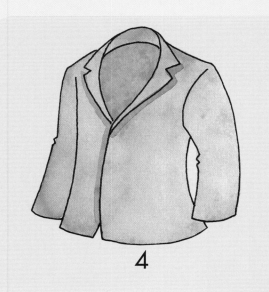

4

Skill: Represent quantities 1–4 by drawing

Picnic on the Beach

Can you find people in groups of 3?

Circle each group
of 3 people you see.

Skill: Identify sets of 3

Up a Tree!

Circle the number that tells how many.

 5　　4　　3

 2　　4　　5

 3　　2　　1

 5　　3　　4

Skill: Determine quantity in sets up to 5

Bunches of Bugs

Look at all the bugs.

Draw lines to connect groups that have the same number of bugs.

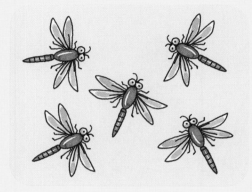

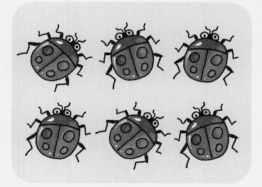

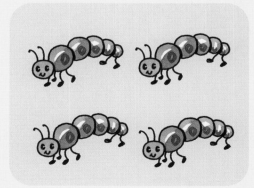

Skill: Match equivalent sets of 4–6

41

Ready to Ride

Are there enough bikes?

Count to see.   Yes   No

Parents: Extra credit! Ask your child to explain how he or she arrived at the answer. Did your child count children and bikes? Draw lines between them? Estimate?

Skill: Determine quantity in sets up to 6

Toy Time

How many toys do you see?

Draw a line from the toys to the right number.

6

5

7

Skill: Determine quantity in sets up to 7

Here's the Scoop!

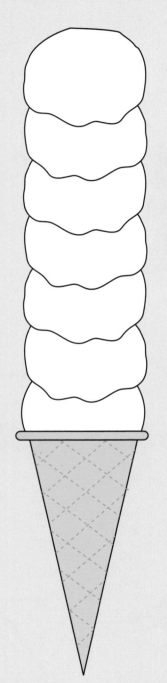

Color 7 scoops.

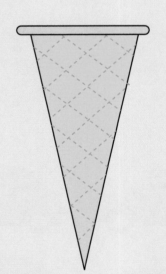

Draw and color
3 scoops.

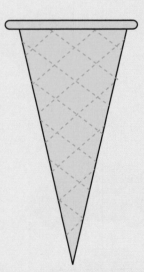

Draw and color
5 scoops.

Skill: Represent quantities 3–7 by drawing

44

How My Garden Grows!

Color 6 flowers yellow.

Color 3 butterflies purple.

Color 9 apples red.

Skill: Represent quantities 3–9 by coloring

Jungle Fun

Circle 8 monkeys.  Circle 8 birds.

Circle 8 butterflies.

Skill: Count to 8 to determine quantity

46

Party Time!

Circle 10 hats. Circle 10 gifts.

Circle 10 cupcakes.

Parents: Extra credit! Ask your child to count how many children and adults there are at the party.

Skill: Count to 10 to determine quantity

49

Rainy Day!

Circle the number that tells how many.

8   10   9   8   7   5   4   5   3

6   7   8   2   4   3   1   2   3

Parents: Extra credit! Ask your child to count how many people are in the picture.

Skill: Count to 10 to determine quantity

50

At the Pond

Circle 9 ducks.   Circle 9 frogs.

Circle 9 dragonflies.

Skill: Count to 9 to determine quantity

52

Clean Up!

Where does each block go?

Draw a line to show.

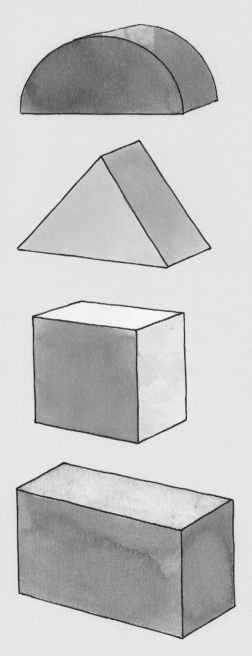

Squares Everywhere!

Connect the blue dots to make a square.

Can you use the red dot in the middle of the square to draw more squares?

How many squares did you make? ☐

Tracing Triangles

Connect the blue dots to make a triangle.

Now use the red dots below to make your own triangles.

How many triangles did you make?

Squares for Bears

These bears like squares! Help them find the squares.

Color all the squares blue.

Skill: Recognize and distinguish squares from other shapes

Searching for Circles!

How many circles can you see?

Circle all of them.

How many did you find?

Skill: Recognize the circle shape

A Shapely Circus!

How many shapes do you see? Write the number.

Shapes at the Shore

Color the shapes!

Color the squares yellow.

Color the rectangles red.

Color the circles orange.

Color the triangles blue.

In Which Case?

Help the musicians find their instrument cases.

Draw a line from each instrument to its case.

Skill: Match objects based on shape

Go-Togethers!

What goes together?

Draw lines to show.

Skill: Sort by use

More Go-Togethers!

Find two things that go together in each row.

Circle them.

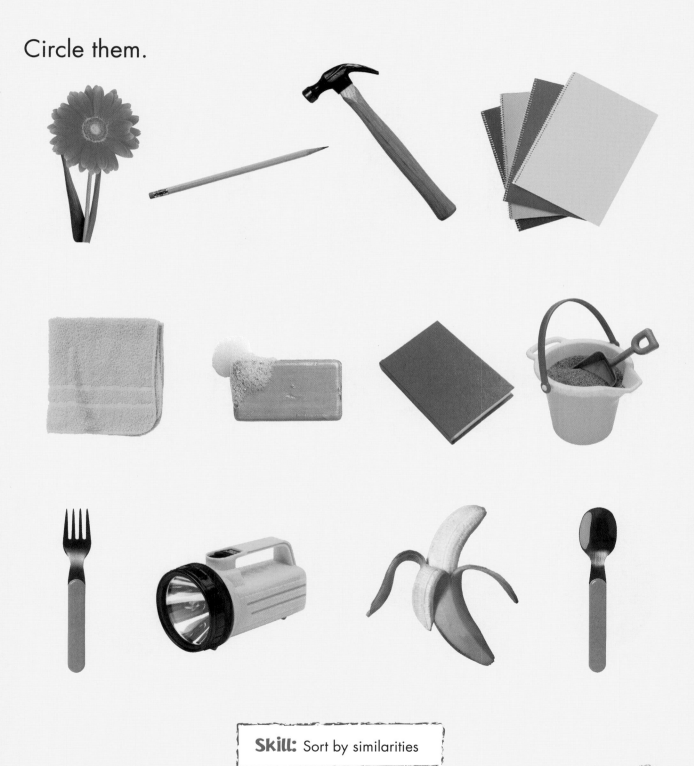

63

What Doesn't Belong?

One thing doesn't belong in each row.

Mark an X through it.

Something's Silly

Find 5 silly things that don't belong in this scene.

Circle them.

Heading for Home!

Help the animals find their homes.

Draw a line from each animal to its home.

Legs, Legs, Legs!

Color all the animals with 4 legs brown.

Color all the animals with 2 legs yellow.

Parents: Extra credit! Ask your child to count the 2-legged animals, the 4-legged animals, and then all the animals.

Skill: Classify by 1 attribute

Shorts! Shirts! Shoes!

Sort the shorts, shirts, and shoes into 3 groups.

Paste photocopies of each group in 1 box.

Parents: Please photocopy and cut out the 9 boxes for your child to sort and paste on page 68.

Skill: Sort by 1 attribute

Who Uses What?

Which worker uses which tool?

Draw lines to show.

Skill: Compare and sort objects by use

Add Another!

Can you think of something else that could go in each group?

Draw it!

Hats Off!

Which hat matches which outfit?

Draw lines to show.

Skill: Recognize and match patterns

Rows of Colors

Can you finish the color patterns in these blocks and beads?

Color to show what comes next.

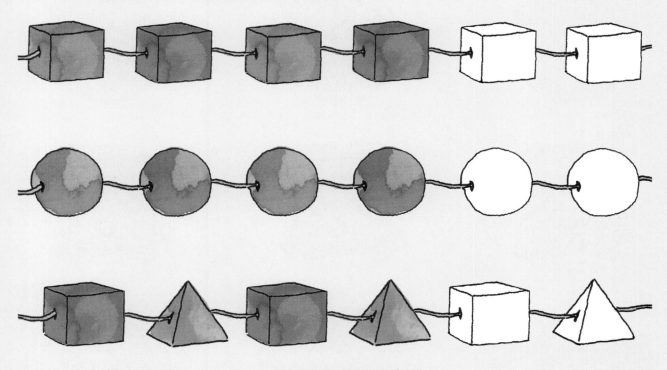

Now make up your own pattern! Color it.

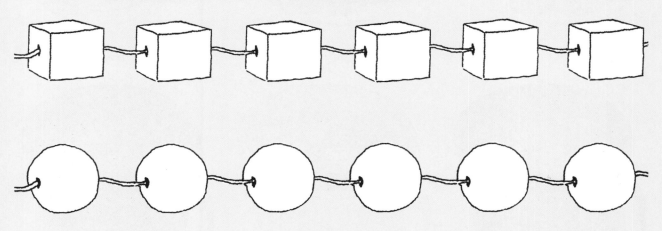

Skills: Continue color patterns; make up a color pattern

Bucketful of Buttons!

What color comes next? Color to show.

75

Can You Find It?

Find this pattern in the picture. Circle it.

Sock Drawer

Find the socks with these patterns. How many are there?
Write the number.

Parade of Shapes

What shape comes next? Draw it, and color it!

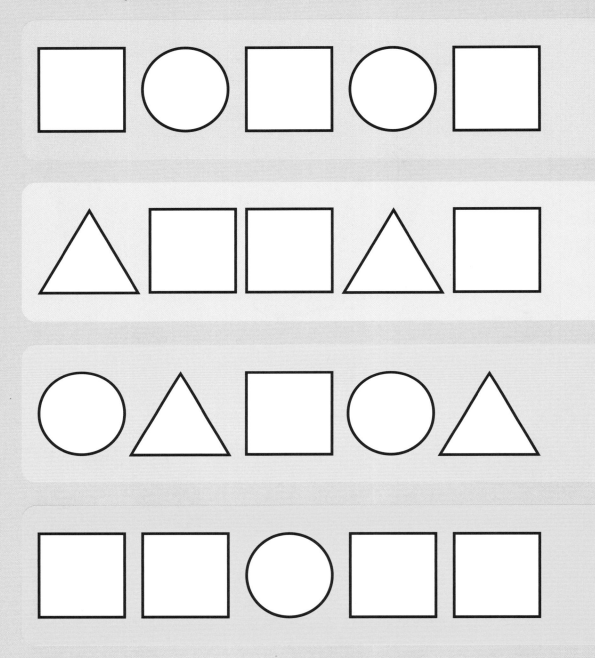

Parents: Extra credit! Ask your child to color all the squares blue, all the circles red, and all the triangles yellow.

Skill: Continue a shape pattern

Small Fry

Circle the picture that is smaller than the first one.

Skill: Compare size to determine what is smaller

Biggest of All

Put an X on the biggest dinosaur in each row.

Skill: Compare size to determine biggest

Big Rigs

Circle the picture that is bigger than the first one.

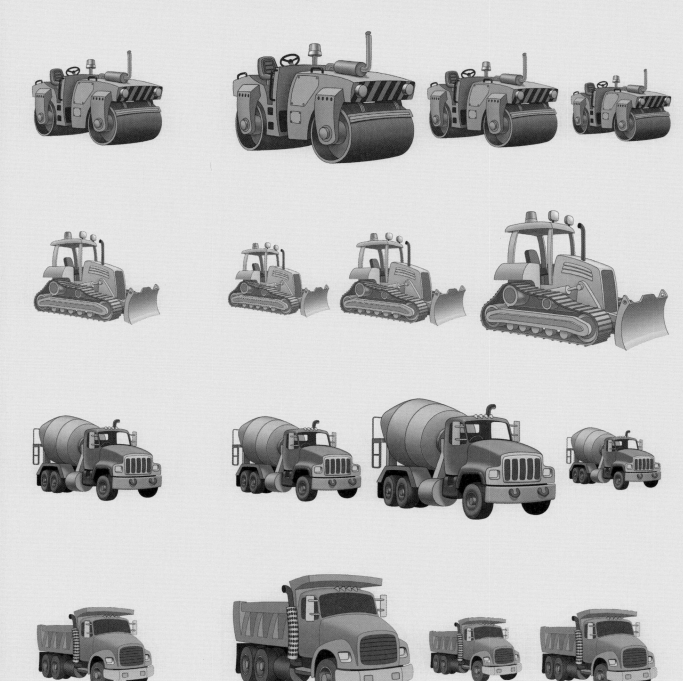

81

Who's Hungry?

Color the smallest piece of food in each row.

Skill: Compare size to determine smallest

Simply the Same Size!

There are 2 things in each row that are the same size.

Circle them.

The Long and Short of It

Which is the longest? Draw a line under it.

Skill: Compare size to determine which is longer

Tip-top Tall

Circle the tallest girl.   Circle the tallest giraffe.

Circle the tallest tree.

Parents: Extra credit! Ask your child to put an X on the shortest girl, giraffe, and tree.

Skill: Compare size to determine which is taller

At the Dog Show!

It is time to start the show.

Paste each dog in its place.

Parents: Photocopy and cut out the 3 show dogs for your child to paste on the page.

Skill: Order by size

Fishy Friends

Color the first fish in each row green.

Color the last fish in each row yellow.

Skill: Determine first and last in an ordered group

Spin Your Wheels

Circle the first object in each row,
and mark an X on the third object.

Animals on Parade

Draw a line under the second animal in each row, and draw a box around the fourth animal.

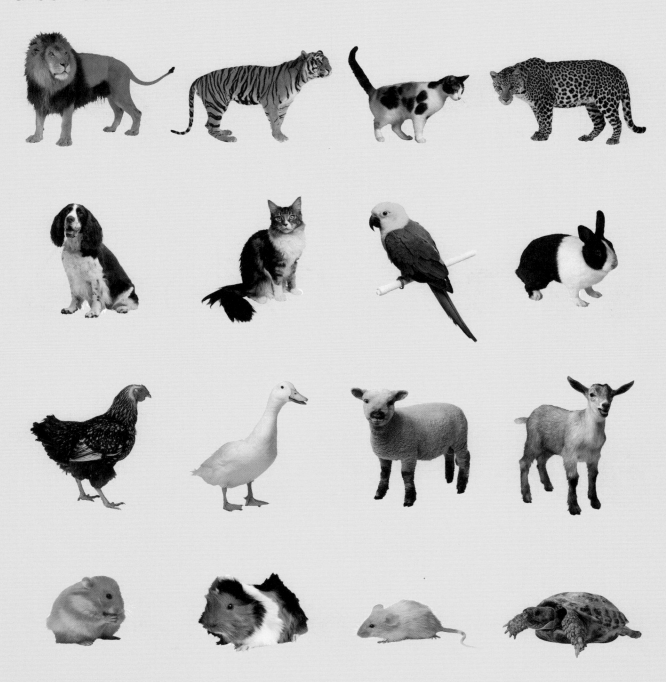

90

Crossing the Finish Line!

Who will finish first? Second? Third?

Draw lines to show the ribbon the first runner, the second runner, and the third runner will get.

Skill: Determine first, second, and third in an ordered group

Walking the Dogs!

Which dog walker is walking the most dogs?
Color that dog walker's shirt red.

Which dog walker is walking the fewest dogs?
Color that dog walker's shirt blue.

Skill: Compare sets to determine which has most and which has fewest

93

Going Swimming!

Which group in each row has more? Circle it!

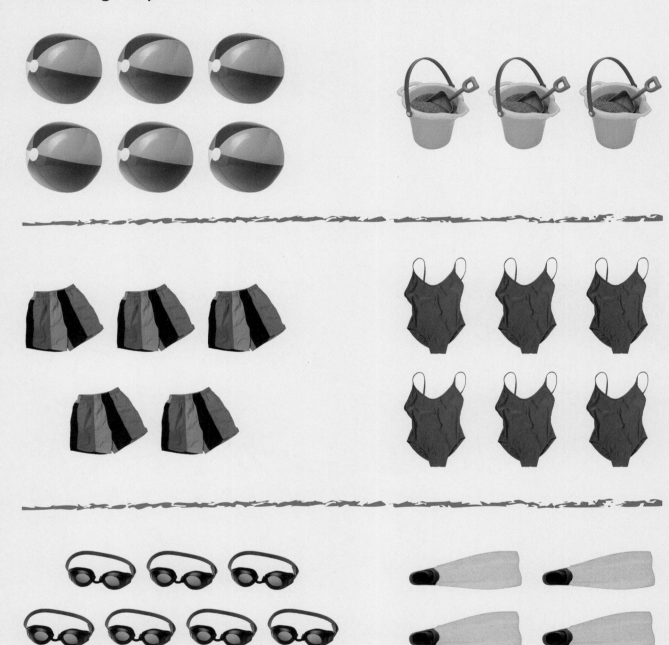

Play Ball!

Which group has less? Draw a square around it.

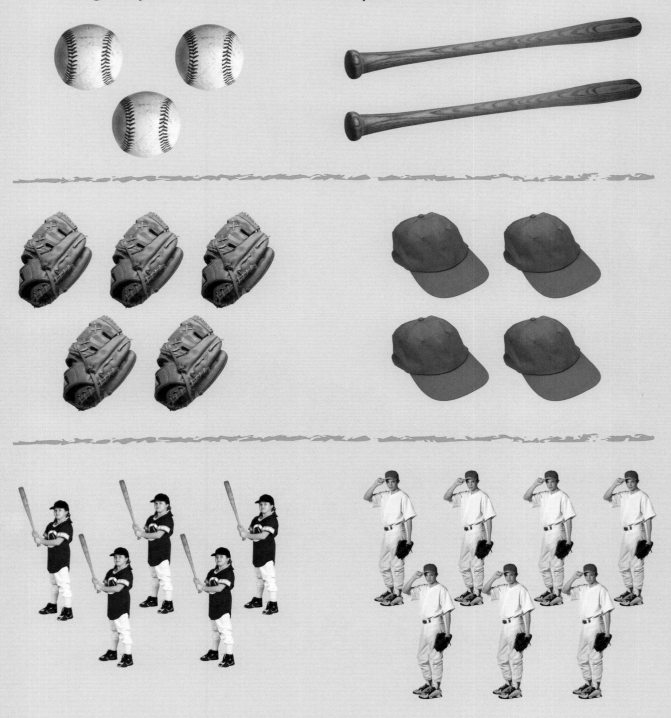

Down by the Pond

Which mom has the fewest babies?

Color her brown.

Skill: Compare sets to determine which has least

Farm Friends

Which groups have the same number of animals?

Draw lines to connect groups that have the same number.

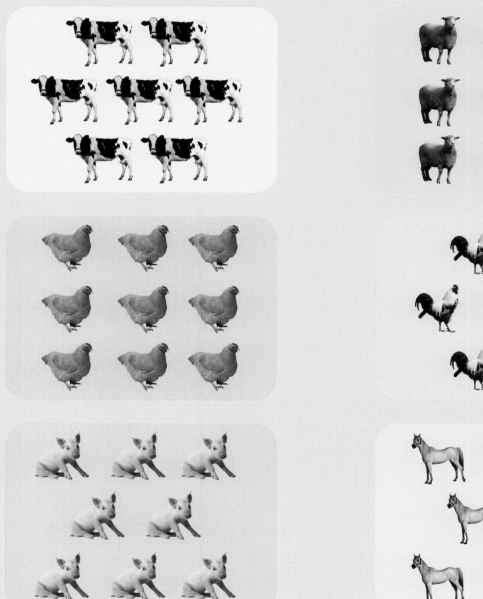

97

Apple Picking

Count the apples on the tree.

Draw the same number of apples on the other tree.

Parents: Extra credit! Ask your child to count how many apples there are all together on both trees!

Your child can also count the apples in the full basket and draw the same number of apples in the empty basket.

Skill: Demonstrate knowledge of equivalent sets by drawing

Taking Time

Which activity takes a longer time? Circle it.

Which activity takes a longer time? Circle it.

Skill: Compare events to determine longer duration

99

That Was Quick!

Which activity takes a shorter time? Circle it.

Which activity takes a shorter time? Circle it.

Skill: Compare events to determine shorter duration

Now Is the Time!

Which things can be used to measure time? Color them.

Skill: Recognize devices that measure time

First Things First

Circle the thing in each row that happens first.

Parents: Extra credit! After the first event in each sequence has been circled, invite your child to tell you what happens next and what happens last.

Skill: Determine what happens first in a sequence

102

What's Next?

Draw lines from the first row to show what happens next.

Skill: Determine what happens next in a sequence

Last of All

What happens last in each row? Draw a square around it.

Parents: Extra credit! Invite your child to label each set of pictures 1, 2, and 3 to show what happened first, next, and last.

Skill: Determine what happens last in a sequence

Let It Grow!

Number the pictures from 1 to 5 to show the order in which they happen.

Skill: Sequence a set of events

Cats! Cats! Cats!

Color the cat inside the box black.

Color the cat behind the box brown.

Color the cat in front of the box yellow.

Color the cat next to the box orange.

Skill: Recognize positional words: *inside, behind, in front of, next to*

Desk Work

Color the things that belong on top of the desk blue.

Color the things that belong under the desk yellow.

Skill: Recognize positional words: *on top of, under*

A Bear's Chair!

Draw something red on top of the bear's chair.

Draw something purple under the bear's chair.

Skill: Demonstrate knowledge of positional words *on top of* and *under* by drawing.

Chest of Toys!

How many toys are inside the toy chest? _____

How many toys are outside the toy chest? _____

Write the numbers.

Parents: Extra credit! Ask your child if there are more toys inside or outside of the chest.

Skill: Recognize positional words: *inside, outside*

Pennies!

A penny is worth 1¢.

How many pennies?

1   2   3

How much is this worth?

1¢   2¢   3¢

How many pennies?

2   3   4

How much is this worth?

2¢   3¢   4¢

How many pennies?

3   4   5

How much is this worth?

3¢   4¢   5¢

How many pennies?

5   6   7

How much is this worth?

5¢   6¢   7¢

Skill: Recognizing the value of a penny

110

Nickels!

A nickel is worth 5¢.

How many nickels?

1   2   3

How much is this worth?

5¢   10¢   15¢

How many nickels?

1   2   3

How much is this worth?

5¢   10¢   15¢

How many nickels?

3   4   5

How much is this worth?

15¢   20¢   25¢

How many nickels?

3   4   5

How much is this worth?

15¢   20¢   25¢

Skill: Recognizing the value of a nickel

111

Dimes!

A dime is worth 10¢.

How many dimes?

1   2   3

How much is this worth?

10¢   20¢   30¢

How many dimes?

2   3   4

How much is this worth?

20¢   30¢   40¢

How many dimes?

2   3   4

How much is this worth?

20¢   30¢   40¢

How many dimes?

4   5   6

How much is this worth?

40¢   50¢   60¢

Skill: Recognizing the value of a dime

Exact Change

Which group of coins shows the exact price? Circle it.

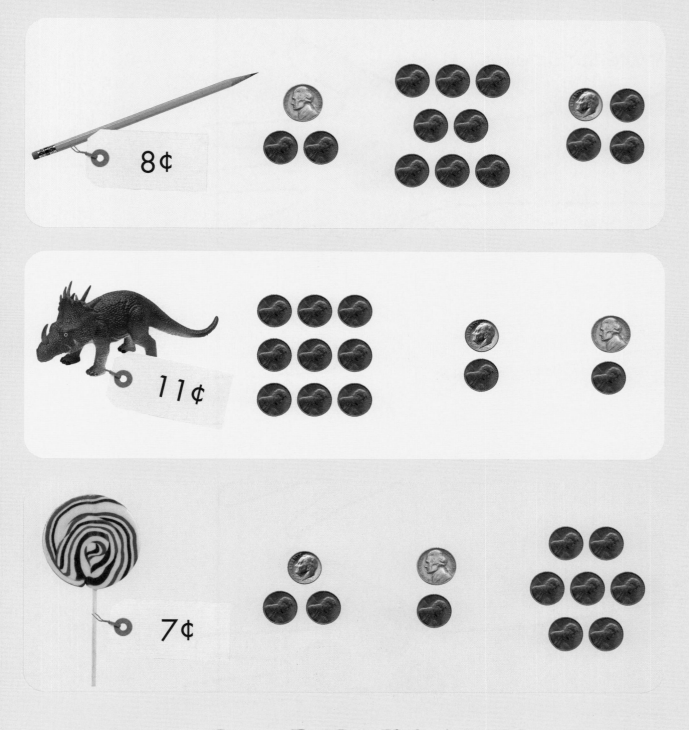

8¢

11¢

7¢

Skill: Match a price with the correct group of coins

Pocket Change

How much money does each child have?

Write the amount.

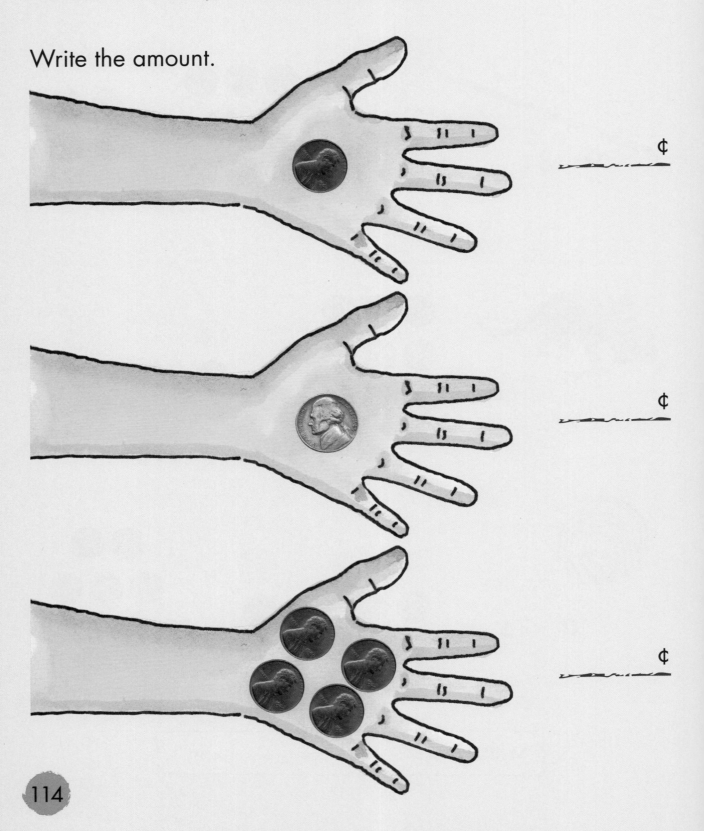

_____ ¢

_____ ¢

_____ ¢

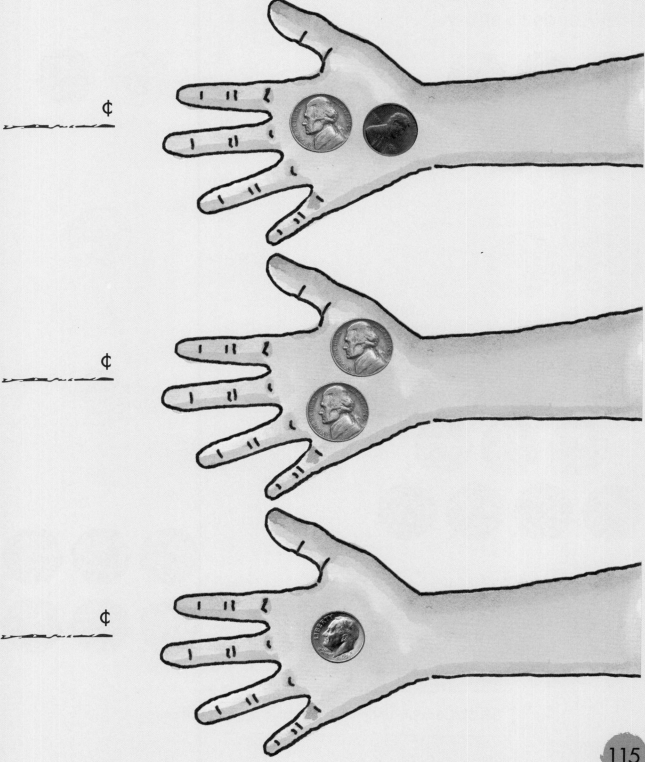

_____ ¢

_____ ¢

_____ ¢

What's It Worth?

Which groups have the same amount of money?

Draw lines to show.

Skill: Compute and match the value of groups of coins

Prices of Prizes!

Which costs most in each row? Circle it.

Skill: Recognize more and less in numbers representing price

How Many Horses?

How many horses are there?

Guess. _____

Now count. _____

How close was your guess?

Parents: Estimating is making an educated guess about an amount of objects.

Skill: Estimate and then count to verify

Counting Cows

How many cows have spots? Guess.

How many cows have no spots? Guess.

Write your guesses on the chart below.

	Solid	Spots
My Guess		
How Many		

Now count. Write the correct numbers on the chart.

Skill: Estimate and record answers on a chart

Toy Store!

How many are there of each toy? Guess.

Write your guesses on the chart.

My Guess				
How Many				

Now count. Write the numbers on the chart.

Skill: Estimate and record answers on a chart

Stripes and Spots

How many animals have stripes?

How many animals have spots?

Color 1 box for each animal.

Skill: Display information about 2 groups on a graph

121

Fresh Fruit

How many apples are there?

How many oranges are there?

How many bananas are there?

Color 1 box for each fruit.

Skill: Display information about 3 groups on a graph

Tick Tock

Color the big hand orange.

Color the little hand blue.

What Time Is It?

The little hand tells the hour.

Circle the number the little hand is pointing to.

2   3   12

1   6   2

9   3   8

1   12   11

Skill: Determine the hour a clock displays

It's That Time of Day!

Is it morning, noon, or night?

Draw lines to match each clock with the right picture.

Lunch Time

Good Night

Rise and Shine

Skill: Match time as shown on a clock with time of day

Bedtime

What time do you go to bed? Write the time. _____

Now draw hands on the clock to show the time!

Skill: Demonstrate knowledge of clock time through drawing

Congratulations

_____

is on the way
to becoming a

Great Math
Student!

Keep up the
good work!

_____